RACHMANINOFF

ALSO AVAILABLE IN THE REALLY EASY PIANO SERIES...

ABBA
25 GREAT HITS. ORDER NO. AM980430

CHILDREN'S FAVOURITES
20 POPULAR HITS. ORDER NO. AM998745

CHRISTMAS
24 FESTIVE CHART HITS. ORDER NO. AM980496

CLASSICAL FAVOURITES
24 WELL-KNOWN FAVOURITES. ORDER NO. AM993366

COLDPLAY
20 SONGS FROM COLDPLAY. ORDER NO. AM989593

ELTON JOHN
24 CLASSIC SONGS. ORDER NO. AM987844

FRANK SINATRA
21 CLASSIC SONGS. ORDER NO. AM987833

GREAT FILM SONGS
22 BIG FILM HITS. ORDER NO. AM993344

GREAT SHOWSTOPPERS
20 POPULAR STAGE SONGS. ORDER NO. AM993355

JAZZ GREATS
22 JAZZ FAVOURITES. ORDER NO. AM1000857

LOVE SONGS
22 CLASSIC LOVE SONGS. ORDER NO. AM989582

MICHAEL JACKSON
19 CLASSIC HITS. ORDER NO. AM1000604

MORE 21ST CENTURY HITS
21 POPULAR HITS. ORDER NO. AM996534

MOZART
22 CLASSICAL FAVOURITES. ORDER NO. AM1000648

NEW CHART HITS
19 BIG CHART HITS. ORDER NO. AM996523

NO. 1 HITS
22 POPULAR CLASSICS. ORDER NO. AM993388

POP HITS
22 GREAT SONGS. ORDER NO. AM980408

SHOWSTOPPERS
24 STAGE HITS. ORDER NO. A M982784

TV HITS
25 POPULAR HITS. ORDER NO. AM985435

60S HITS
25 CLASSIC HITS. ORDER NO. AM985402

70S HITS
25 CLASSIC SONGS. ORDER NO. AM985413

80S HITS
25 POPULAR HITS. ORDER NO. AM985424

90S HITS
24 POPULAR HITS. ORDER NO. AM987811

50 FABULOUS SONGS
FROM POP SONGS TO CLASSICAL THEMES. ORDER NO. AM999449

50 GREAT SONGS
FROM POP SONGS TO CLASSICAL THEMES. ORDER NO. AM995643

50 HIT SONGS
FROM POP HITS TO JAZZ CLASSICS. ORDER NO. AM1000615

PIANO TUTOR
FROM FIRST STEPS TO PLAYING IN A WIDE
RANGE OF STYLES — FAST!. ORDER NO. AM996303

ALL TITLES CONTAIN BACKGROUND NOTES FOR EACH SONG PLUS
PLAYING TIPS AND HINTS.

PUBLISHED BY
HAL LEONARD.

EXCLUSIVE DISTRIBUTORS:
HAL LEONARD
7777 WEST BLUEMOUND ROAD
MILWAUKEE, WI 53213
EMAIL: INFO@HALLEONARD.COM

HAL LEONARD EUROPE LIMITED
42 WIGMORE STREET
MARYLEBONE, LONDON, W1U 2RY
EMAIL: INFO@HALLEONARDEUROPE.COM

HAL LEONARD AUSTRALIA PTY. LTD.
4 LENTARA COURT
CHELTENHAM, VICTORIA, 3192 AUSTRALIA
EMAIL: INFO@HALLEONARD.COM.AU

ORDER NO. AM1008722
ISBN 978-1-78305-513-5
THIS BOOK © COPYRIGHT 2014 BY HAL LEONARD.

MUSIC ARRANGED BY BARRIE CARSON TURNER.
EDITED BY JENNI NOREY.
PRINTED IN THE EU.

WWW.HALLEONARD.COM

Etudes-tableaux, Op.33
VIII. Moderato

Composed by Sergei Rachmaninoff

Rachmaninoff wrote two sets of 'Etudes-tableaux', Op.33 and Op.39, and this moody, sombre piece is number eight from Op.33. Only six from this set were initially published in 1911, the third and fifth being published after the composer's death.

Hints & Tips: The quaver pattern passes between the right and left hand throughout and needs to be kept smooth and fluent.

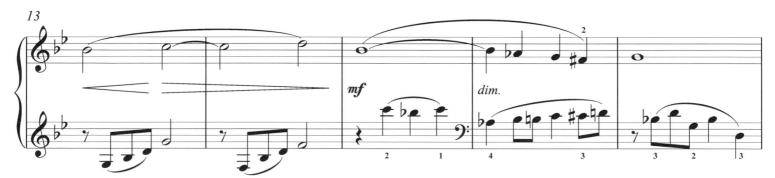

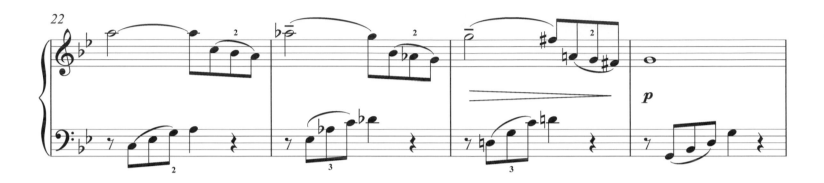

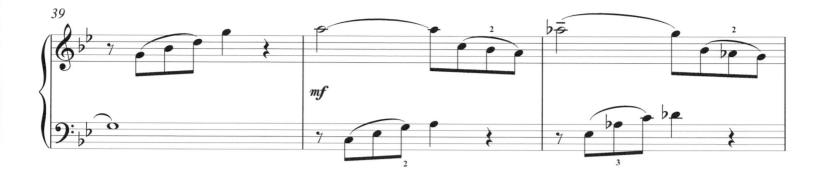

Aleko
XI. Intermezzo
Composed by Sergei Rachmaninoff

The Bolshoi Theatre's premiere of Rachmaninoff's first opera *Aleko* was in Moscow in 1893, a performance which was attended by Tchaikovsky. The libretto, written by Vladimir Nemirovich-Danchenko, was adapted from Alexander Pushkin's poem *The Gypsies*.

Hints & Tips: In this piece the time signature changes from compound (6/8) to simple (3/4) but the tempo remains the same. Practise these changes until the transitions are smooth.

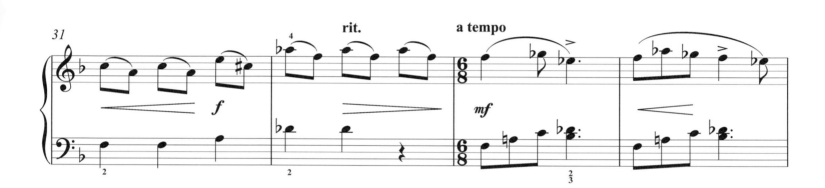

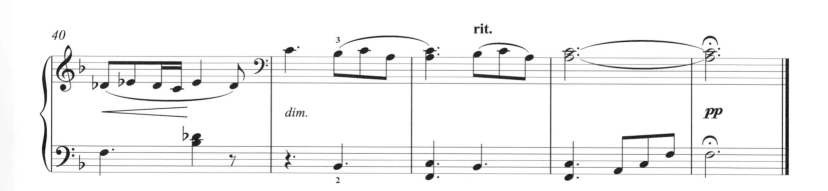

Élégie
No.1 from 'Morceaux de Fantasie', Op.3
Composed by Sergei Rachmaninoff

'Élégie' is the first of five 'Morceaux de Fantasie' (fantasy pieces). The fantasy here refers more to the imagery of the works, rather than the structure of the music. This collection of pieces was dedicated to Rachmaninoff's harmony teacher, Anton Arensky.

Hints & Tips: The left hand rhythms are steady and simple; this will help with counting the notes tied over the bar lines in the right hand.

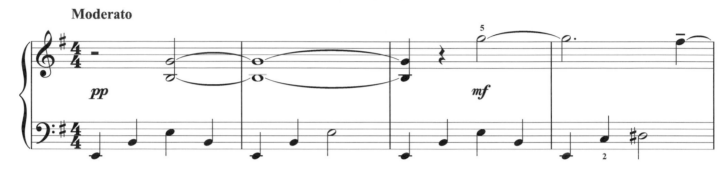

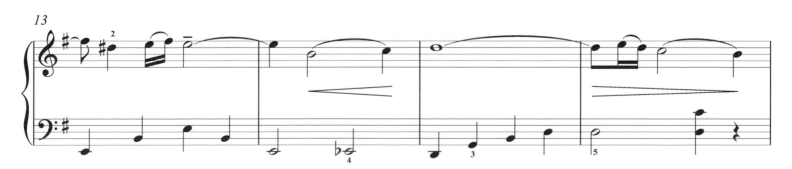

Fragments
(ii/19/3)

Composed by Sergei Rachmaninoff

This short piece was one of Rachmaninoff's last compositions for piano. Written in 1917, it was first published in the U.S. music magazine *The Etude* in 1919.

Hints & Tips: Another piece with changing time signatures to be wary of! Make sure you look through carefully and make a note of all the changes before you begin.

Andante semplice

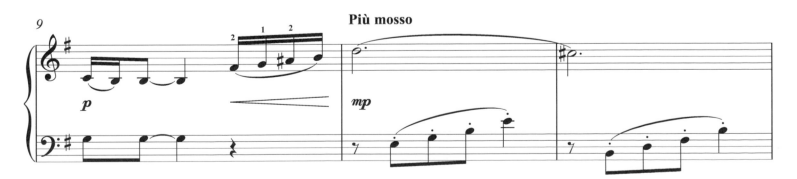

Nocturne
No.1 from '7 Morceaux de salon', Op.10

Composed by Sergei Rachmaninoff

This is the first of seven 'Morceaux de Salon' (salon pieces) for solo piano, which were written between 1893 and 1894. 'Nocturne' includes suggestions of both Tchaikovsky and Chopin in its composition.

Hints & Tips: This piece is full of accidentals, so be very careful. Practising some chromatic scales will help with the fingering.

Andante espressivo

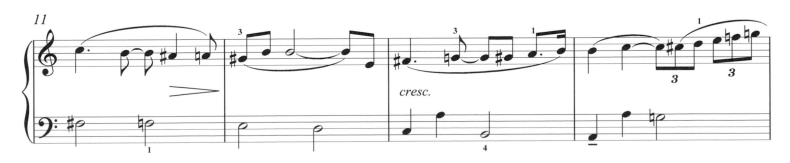

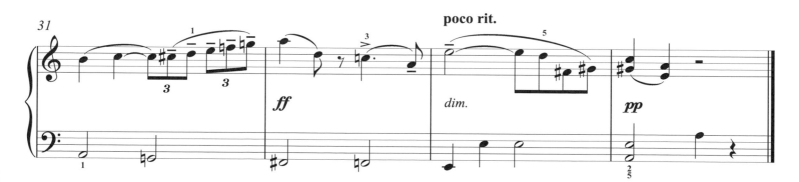

Moments musicaux, Op.16
III. Andante cantabile
Composed by Sergei Rachmaninoff

Taken from a set of six contrasting pieces, each representing a different musical form, this cross between a song without words and a funeral march has been described as being characteristically the "most Russian" of the group.

Hints & Tips: Changing time signatures, accidentals, dynamics- there's a lot to look out for in this. Practise separate hands a section at a time, then slowly put it all together.

Andante cantabile ♩ = 56

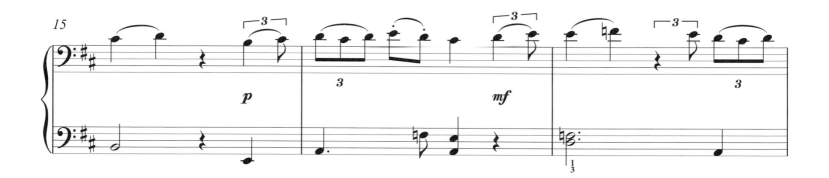

a tempo   D.S. al Coda

⊕ Coda   rit.

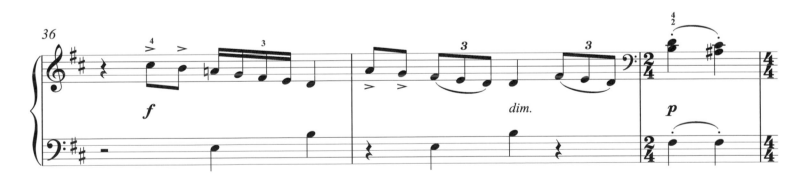

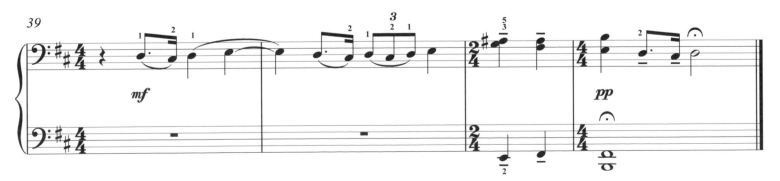

Piano Concerto No.2
2nd Movement

Composed by Sergei Rachmaninoff

A performance of the second and third movements of Rachmaninoff's second piano concerto was given in 1900, with the composer on piano. However, the work was not premiered in its entirety until 1901, again with the composer as the soloist.

Hints & Tips: It is marked *dolce e sempre espressivo* (literally *sweetly and always expressively*) at the start, so really make the most of the dynamics and performance directions!

Piano Concerto No.3
1st Movement

Composed by Sergei Rachmaninoff

The first movement from Rachmaninoff's third piano concerto, this was used prominently in the film *Shine*, which was based on the life of Australian concert pianist David Helfgott.

Hints & Tips: Pay attention to the phrasing in this. Don't let it drag and keep the melody flowing.

Allegro ma non tanto ♩ = 112

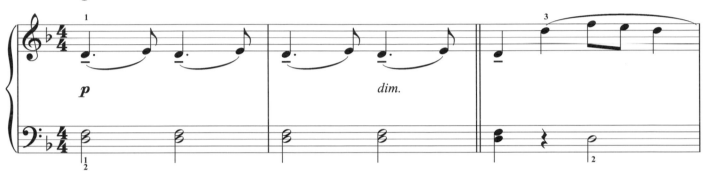

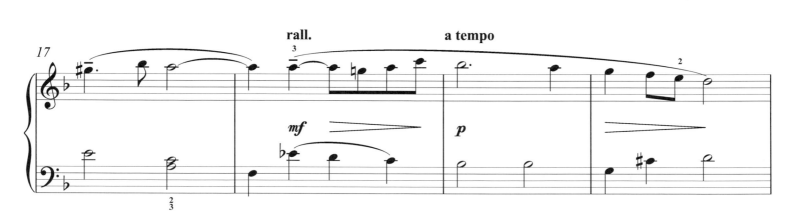

Piano Sonata No.2, Op.36
2nd Movement

Composed by Sergei Rachmaninoff

The original version of this 1913 three-movement sonata lasted roughly 25 minutes. Rachmaninoff reworked it in 1931, the new arrangement lasting around 19 minutes, with the added note "The new version, revised and reduced by author."

Hints & Tips: Careful counting is needed here when the time signature changes in bar 7, with a pick-up into the 12/8 section.

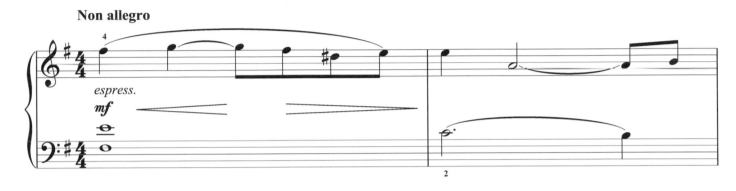

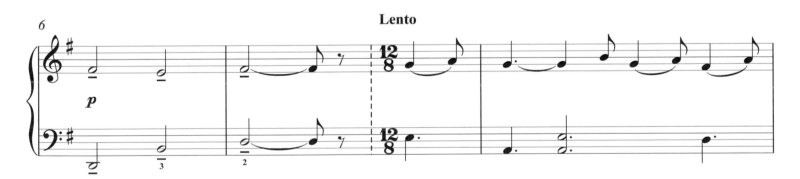

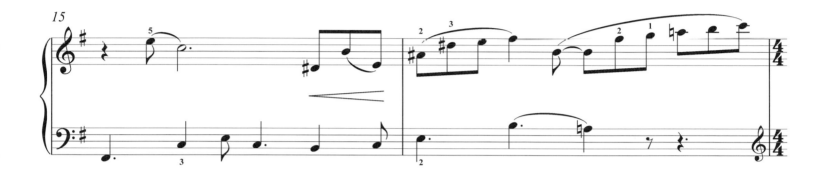

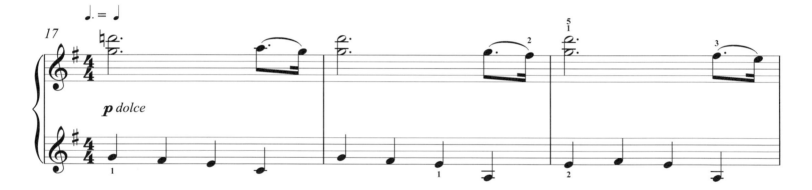

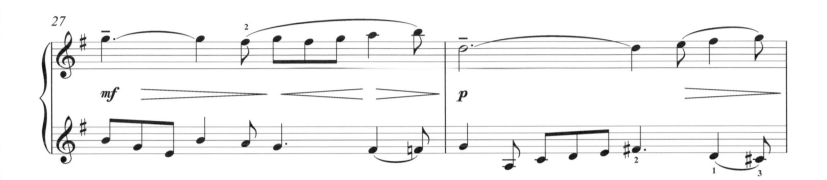

Prélude
No.2 from 'Morceaux de Fantasie', Op.3

Composed by Sergei Rachmaninoff

Of all the pieces from 'Morceaux de Fantasie', 'Prélude' (originally in C sharp minor) is the most famous and was singled out at the premiere in 1892, the review of the work stating that it "aroused enthusiasm".

Hints & Tips: Articulation is important throughout this piece. Don't be tempted to start too fast, as the tempo increases in bar 14 for the *Agitato* section.

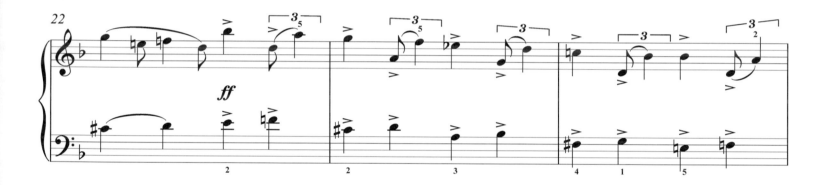

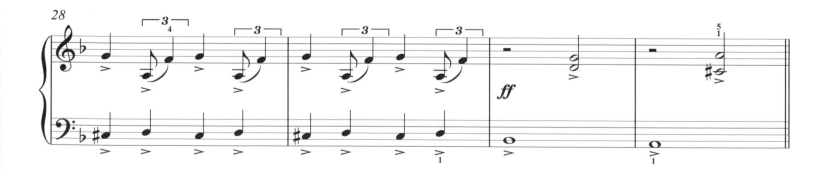

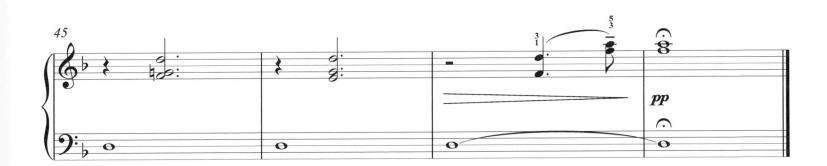

Preludes, Op.23
V. Alla marcia

Composed by Sergei Rachmaninoff

Even though it was written two years earlier, this *Alla marcia* was included in the Op.23 preludes which were finally completed in 1903. It is the most famous of the collection and the one that has been recorded the most.

Hints & Tips: The march-like feel is established straight away with the quaver, quaver, crotchet rhythm in the right hand, which occurs through the whole piece. Make sure the quavers are even each time.

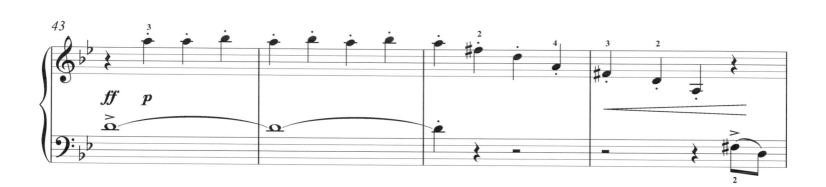

Tempo primo

Preludes, Op.32
XII. Allegro
Composed by Sergei Rachmaninoff

Rachmaninoff's 13 Op.32 compositions completed his earlier preludes (Op.23 and the C sharp minor prelude) to make a full set of 24 preludes in all major and minor keys.

Hints & Tips: It would be easy for the left hand to be overshadowed by the higher pitched right hand. Make sure it comes through.

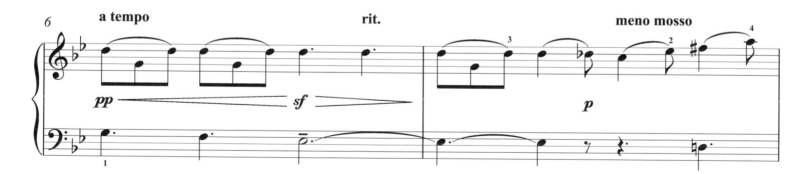

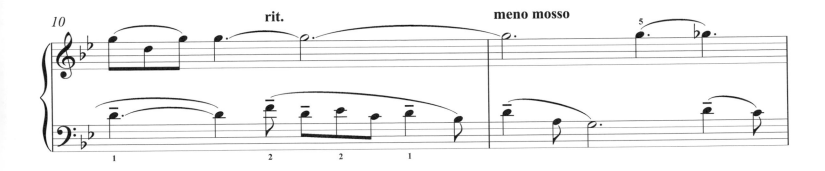

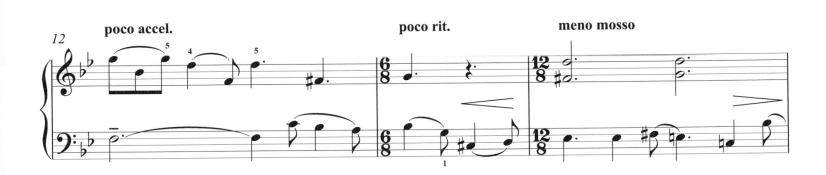

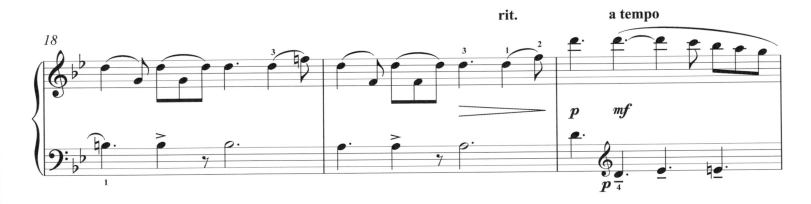

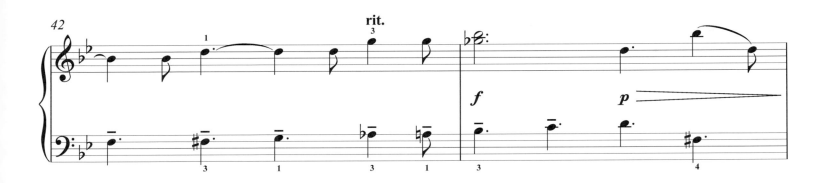

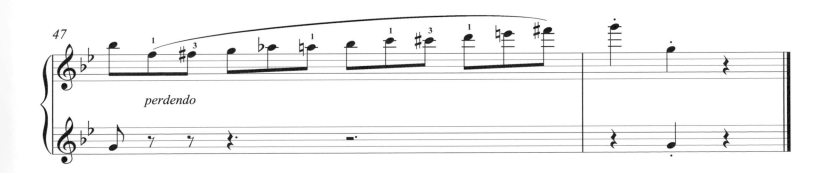

Rhapsody On A Theme Of Paganini

Composed by Sergei Rachmaninoff

Based on the 'Caprice No.24' for solo violin, variations on Paganini's work has also been done by Brahms and Liszt, but Rachmaninoff's remains the most memorable; in particular the 18th variation, which can be seen here from bar 25.

Hints & Tips: Note the different sections and different feels. The 'Theme' at the start is fast and energetic, in contrast to the variation from bar 25 onwards, which is slow and expressive.

Theme
Allegro vivace

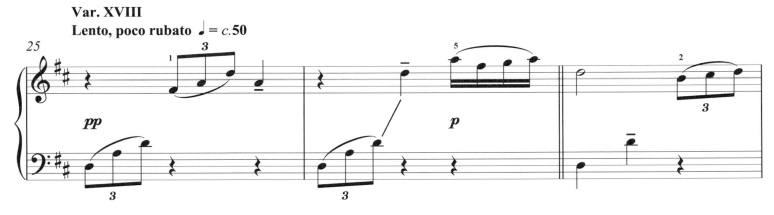

Var. XVIII
Lento, poco rubato ♩ = *c.***50**

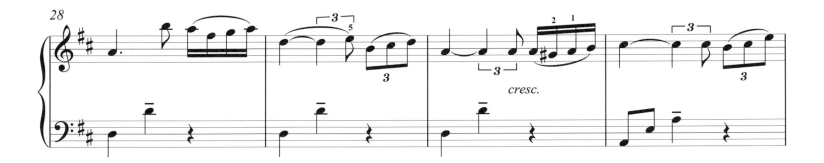

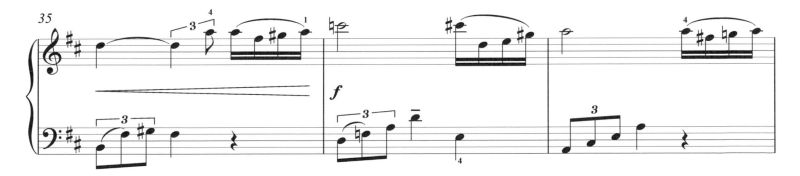

Symphonic Dances
1st Movement

Composed by Sergei Rachmaninoff

Originally called 'Fantastic Dances', the suite was composed for full orchestra, though Rachmaninoff also did an arrangement for two pianos. Several themes from his earlier works appear throughout, and this being Rachmaninoff's final composition, it makes for a fitting conclusion to his musical career.

Hints & Tips: The driving rhythm needs to be kept moving. Practise with a metronome, starting at a slower tempo if necessary and building up to the correct speed.

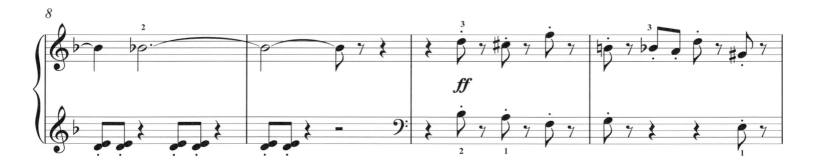

molto marcato

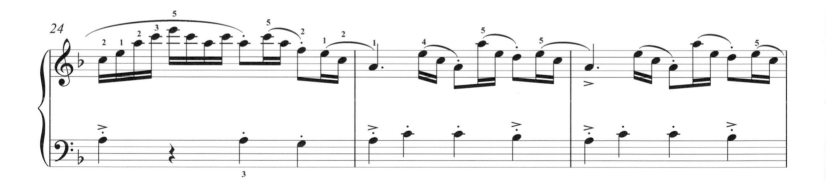

41

Symphony No.2
3rd Movement

Composed by Sergei Rachmaninoff

After the disappointing reaction to his first symphony, Rachmaninoff's second was more favourably received. The theme in the slow third movement is mainly played by the first violin, echoed by a solo clarinet and the full oboe section.

Hints & Tips: Use the dynamics to make the melody in the right hand really expressive, while the left provides a soft accompaniment.

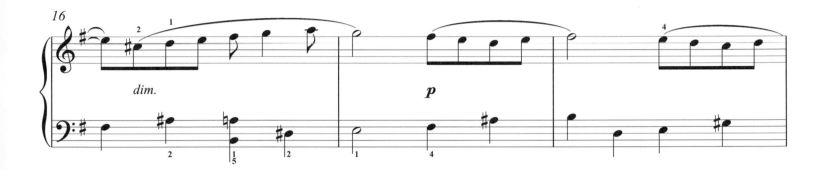

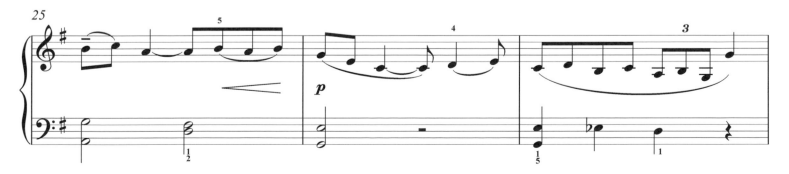

poco a poco cresc.

dim.

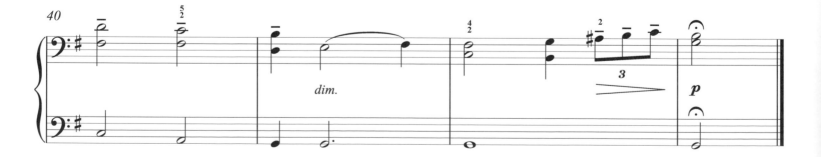

Vocalise
No.14 from 'Fourteen Songs', Op.34

Composed by Sergei Rachmaninoff

This song without words was written for soprano or tenor voice and piano accompaniment. It is sung using only one vowel, of the singer's choosing- most usually 'ah'. Many arrangements have been done, with various instruments in place of the vocal melody.

Hints & Tips: Remember that the melody was written for the voice, so really let it sing!

47

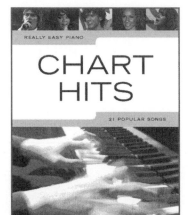

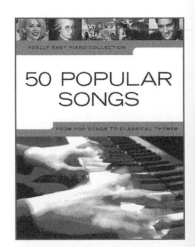